Body Language Training

How To Attract Any Woman You Want!

Get Women Using Respect, Power and Nonverbal Communication

Robert Moore

Robert Moore

Table of Contents

Robert Moore

Introduction

Hey badass!

I want to thank you and congratulate you for purchasing *Body Language Training*.

You should know that human beings are constantly reading situations and other people so that, really quickly, they can know what category put them in: high status, middle status, or low status.

It's just a survival mechanism, because you have to know who has the power and who hasn't. That's something that's been hardwired into us over thousands and thousands of years.

So, most people don't trust words, because we've been taught from a young age to lie with them. Everyone can say: "I drive *that* supercar", "I live in *that* penthouse", "I know *that* person". I mean, everyone can say those words: both high status or lower status individuals.

That's why most people prefer to read those status cues through the body language: THAT is the honest signal! It's not easy to fake and it's easily recognized.

Remember this general law: high status body language = high status person.

It's that simple, and we trust it.

Once we make the decision or opinion about that person it's almost impossible for us to break it.

Therefore, your body language is the UNSPOKEN TRUTH, and you should master it if you want to step up your game and your whole life.

And now, I will show you how to train it in order to become a complete, powerful badass, who appears high status in every situation.

Thank you again for your purchase. Now let's start!

The Foundation For All Things Bad Ass

"Optimism is the faith that leads to achievement. Nothing can be done without hope and confidence." – Helen Keller

If confidence were man, I betcha he'd be one of the most misunderstood ones like, say, Caitlyn Jenner! In fact, most people's perception or impression are often too skewed that only a few people dare to come within 10 feet from it. But not you, Holmes! You want to be an alpha male that draws in the chicks and gets under their pants, right?

That's why you shouldn't fear the concept of confidence but rather embrace it like you would Megan Fox or Mila Kunis if you had both the opportunity and balls to do it. To help you do just that, I'll kick those skewed perceptions in the bum to get it out of your system of a down.

Not to sound all spiritual and self-righteous but one of the best ways I can drive home the importance of having the right thinking about confidence is found in the Bible. Yes, I read it sometimes! It says you can't put new wine in old wines skins –

the ancient way of storing and aging new wines. Why? It says – and this is scientifically proven – that if you put new wine in an old wineskin, the latter will burst and waste that new wine.

Your mindsets are the wineskins and what you're about to learn about confidence is new wine. It makes perfect sense therefore to replace the old wineskins (mindsets) with new ones that will allow you to receive new impartations that will take your self-confidence level to new heights of glory!

WRONG MINDSETS ABOUT CONFIDENCE

Wrong mindsets or beliefs about confidence, certain mindsets either make you use it wrong or keep you from even pursuing it.

To help you become confident enough to be badass, let's take a look at some of the most common wrong mindsets that can either keep your from wanting to be confident or keep you from using it correctly.

Skewed Perception #1: You Can Just Fake It Until You Make It

Yeah, you heard it before. Act like you're rich and you'll eventually have $1 million in your bank account sooner or later! Nothing can be farther from the truth. If you act rich, you'll need to spend rich! If you spend rich when you're not yet rich, the last thing you'll become is a millionaire. You'll actually end up filing for bankruptcy! Common sense, right?

When it comes to confidence, acting like you are can only get you so far.

Sure, it's a good way to boost your confidence in the short-term and help you start of on the right foot when it comes to genuinely building up your self-confidence but if that's all you're gonna stand on, you might as well not stand on it at all. You need a genuine change from within if you'd like to be really confident and consistently exhibit the right body language for attracting all the chicks you wanna do.

With pirated (read: counterfeit) confidence, you'll probably be able to convince half the people half the time or if you want to be optimistic, all the people all the time.

But believe me, it won't hold water, especially if you're trying to score on a really hot chick. You may act all confident and all that shit but as soon as that chick challenges your "confidence" and "manliness" by making things difficult, you'll eventually fold. Your true, wussy self will eventually show at the cracks until you're the epitome of a Humpty Dumpty: down and broken.

So let's work on your most important organ. No, not your dick! I'm talking about your brain! Change your mind and you can change your life! When you're genuinely confident within, your body language will be naturally consistent and unassailable. You and I know the inevitable result of such body language, right?

Skewed Perception #2: Confidence Is Hubris

Hubris is being overconfident, i.e., self-centered, arrogant, conceited and feeling superior to everyone. As with food and sleep, too much of good things can eventually become bad for your sex life. Agree? I thought so.

Ok, so now that you get that being confident to get chicks isn't hubris, how can you actually determine how much is too much? How I wish there was kind of metric or official Guinness World Record of some sort to refer to but unfortunately, there's none. That doesn't mean that you won't be able to find out if you're confident or arrogant. You can pretty much estimate if you are through the following comparisons.

Interrupting

So when is interrupting more of arrogance or hubris and when is it confidence? If you're in a conversation with someone who has the hots for your baby sister and is talking about how he'd like to bang her and all that sex stuff that hardcore porn movies are made of, interrupting him in the middle of his speech isn't just confident – it's also the right thing to do. Having the guts to displease your close friend in order to defend your little sister's honor is confidence.

If you're with a group of friends and someone was talking about his or her recent meaningful accomplishment and you butt in to introduce your own agenda without giving your friend the benefit of finishing the story, that's hubris or arrogance. That's neither cool nor respectful. It's not safe, either especially if your friend is built like Dwayne "The Rock" Johnson.

Dropping Names

Imagine you were sent by your company's President to represent him in a very important, high-level meeting. When you arrive at the other company's headquarters and you go straight to that company President's office and say "I'm here to meet with Mr. or Ms. So-And-So. I'm representing our company President Mr. or Ms. This-And-That," that isn't name dropping. That's confidence in the authority your company President gave you.

If you're one of the millions of people who are part of the iPhone mega-cult and wanted to score a unit of the latest model on the day of the release itself but found – to your chagrin – that the line at 12:00 midnight is already 2 blocks long, you have 2 choices. Fall in line and camp out or return in the morning, cut to the front of the line and tell the store personnel that "Hey, I know Tim Cook." that's hubris. You're not the only one who knows Tim Cook, you know. Practically everybody in the United States or who is an iPhone cultanatic knows him too. The only question then is does he know you? And even then, you still have no right to cut in line.

Finger Pointing

When your officemate gets promoted despite your dissenting opinion and you point to him saying sincerely "You're the man (or woman)!" that's confidence. Pointing your fingers at an officemate when addressing him or her during a meeting isn't – it's hubris.

Skewed Perception #3: Confidence Is Chutzpah

Pronounced as hutz-pah (the C is silent), it is derived from the Hebrew or Jewish word – surprise – "hut spa" that refers to insolence or audacity. Like hubris, chutzpah is a negative manifestation of confidence in the sense that it exceeds healthy levels of the stuff.

So how do you know if its chutzpah or confidence? As with hubris, I'll show you through examples.

Confidence is requesting a Democrat to vote for a Republican presidential candidate. Chutzpah is mocking or condemning that person for not indulging your request.

Walking up to a hot, beautiful stranger in a bar, starting and keeping an interesting and fun banter and eventually getting her number is confidence. Chutzpah is telling the same girl as you approach her "Why not do yourself a big favor and make sweet love to me?"

Asking a prospective client who just turned down your sales pitch for referrals is confidence. Forcing that prospect to accept your proposal by telling him how screwed his logic for not doing so is and maligning his or her decision making skills is chutzpah.

There are a million other examples I can give you but you get the picture, eh?

Skewed Perception #4: Confidence Means Being Insensitive

You don't have to disregard other people's feelings and opinions by acting and speaking in ways that are offensive, impolite or rude in order to be confident. Again, that's overconfidence. It isn't confident to joke about a person's physical disability in the company of other people – it's insensitivity. Like alcohol, confidence is best in moderate amounts because too little of it isn't useful and too much of it is destructive.

Here are examples that can help clarify the difference between confidence and being plain insensitive.

Speaking Your Mind

When you speak your mind at the proper place, tone, time and in the right words, that's confidence. Take the case of today's flavor of the year: same-sex marriage. Confidence is comfortably expressing your contrasting opinion on the matter when asked by either a religious zealot or a hard-core LGBT fanatic. It takes confidence to respectfully and honestly express a dissenting opinion either way with either of the two extreme people when asked. If you simply express an opinion that will keep you in the graces of the person asking you about it, you're not confident. You're a coward.

Insensitivity is when you're introduced to a same-sex couple and immediately blurt out without batting an eyelash "I believe you're on the highway to hell." When you're introduced to a highly religious person and immediately comment "God's not real. He's just opium for the masses who aren't able to cut it in real life.", that's insensitivity also.

Smoking

Smoking is one of those double-edged swords when it comes to confidence. On one hand, you can't deny the coolness factor it bestows on those who huff and puff until the cig's all burned out. Look no further than the Marlboro Man, one of the most enduring coolness icons of all time. Dying from lung cancer never looked so good, eh? Smoking in the designated areas, despite what people think about it, is confidence. Smoking in non-designated areas and in the presence of non-smokers isn't confidence. It's insensitivity.

I get it, we all have our rights to live or die as we choose. But our rights end where others' begins and sadly, many insensitive people don't know where the line is drawn. It's as if they're the centers of the universe and everyone and everything revolves around them and their rights. Be confident, not insensitive!

TRUE CONFIDENCE IS

Now that we've demolished some of the wrong mindsets that may have prevented you from desiring to be confident, it's now time for the real slim shady to please stand up! I'll help you understand what real confidence is through the lemon tree illustration.

If you plant a lemon seed on the ground, what can you reasonably expect to grow from that patch of land many years from now? That's right – a lemon tree! Very good, Holmes! You've been doing your homework, I see! Why would you expect that to be so? It's quite obvious – a lemon seed can't be expected, reasonably at least, to grow into an apple tree!

Now, imagine with me for a moment that it has been more than a decade since you last visited that planted seed and when you returned, you find that in its place is a lemon tree – with lemons! If you pick all the hanging lemons from its branches, can you expect to harvest lemons again the next season? Why, yes you would! Why? Because it's a lemon tree, Holmes! You would be crazy to expect apples to grow from a lemon tree right?

But what if you graft apples into the branches of the lemon tree so you can harvest apples next year? Or what if you graft apple tree branches into the lemon tree's trunk – can you expect apples to grow from that tree next season or seasons after that?

No. Why? That's right – it's not an apple tree! It's a lemon tree and as such, you can expect it to grow lemons year in and year out.

If you cut the branches, will it still bear lemons? It may take some time but still, yes – it will bear lemons again. Why? Because it's still a lemon tree. What if you cut the trunk? It will still bear lemons in the future, though after a much longer time because the whole tree will practically have to grow back again.

Why such persistence?

What keeps the lemon tree from consistently bearing lemon fruits even if almost fatally mutilated? I mean, it isn't a zombie from The Walking Dead, right?

The answer is its roots. For as long as the roots are alive, the tree will continue to bear fruit – lemon fruits in particular. Until you uproot the thing, it'll continue bearing lemon fruits. It's the same with confidence, Dawg!

If you're confident on the inside (roots), you'll consistently act confident and your body language will unconsciously be that of one who is truly confident. Confident body language can no doubt help you feel confident quickly and may also help make you truly confident but if it's all just for show and you really have no basis for it (roots), your body language (fruits) won't be consistent.

If your true self isn't confident, don't expect yourself to consistently act confident over the long term.

That's why we gonna lay the smack down in terms of a solid foundation from which your legendary high-status body language will stand on for good. It'll be like building your house on solid rock instead of shifting sands, badass!

Robert Moore

Thinking Yourself Confident

"As a man thinks in his heart, so is he."

Frankly, I can't imagine a world without biases. Though I want to live in one, it's just impossible because all of us have different opinions and preferences. As such, no perfect harmony can ever exist and biases will be as sure as death and taxes.

For example, I'd be hard pressed to expect people in the slums of marginalized countries to believe they can rise from the ashes and live a prosperous life if all their lives, they never saw how it is to be prosperous. Not that I don't want to encourage them but I'm leveling my expectations that chances are, I won't be able to. The living conditions in which such people grew up in have created mindsets of poverty for life and as such, they're biased against the idea of getting out debilitating poverty.

Contrast that to other poor people who rose from their abject poverty to become filthy rich! How'd that happen? How did they come to believe and have hope while most people of the same status never got to? It's because some of them were able to catch a glimpse – even a vision – of its reality, that it is possible to rise from poverty into prosperity. Maybe it was a relative, friend or neighbor who was able to do so. The important thing is that they saw it can be done and so they believed they can do so as well. Thus, they're biased against the belief that if you're born poor, you'll die poor.

THE POWER OF THOUGHTS

While it's true that you have no direct control over most of the events in your life such as the family into which you were born, you can control what you think about – whether it's about that hot chick you've been eyeing for the longest time or about the fact you need a lot of work when it comes to scoring with chicks, among other noble goals in life. In particular, you can control the things that come into your subconscious mind, which is the one that's responsible for your habits and attitudes.

Before going deeper into this Freudian mumbo-jumbo thing, allow me to orient you – if you're not yet so – about your mind. It's compartmentalized into two: the conscious and the subconscious. The conscious mind is the one that you use to actively control your movements, thoughts and speech, particularly when you're paying attention or conscious about them. The subconscious mind, on the other hand, is that part of your mind that basically controls your life without having to be aware of it or exercise active control over. These things include breathing, your heart beat, your digestive process and all the other movements you've already mastered like driving, biking and playing the guitar.

The subconscious mind can be thought of as a torpedo. Using your conscious mind, you program the "coordinates" of the targets (goals) you want to achieve and once you do that, you simply fire it and let it do its job of seeking those targets. Like the torpedo, you can't directly control it. You can only re-program it to seek an entirely different set of targets that are more in line with what you really want.

Have you ever experienced trying so hard to do something – perhaps change a behavior or eradicate a habit – differently and only end up frustrated because you keep on reverting back to your old behavior or habit? It's because you're trying to acquire a target by controlling the uncontrollable torpedo instead of re-programming it to acquire a new target. It's like learning how to play guitar for the first time. You can bury your head under all the YouTube lessons you can possibly watch in 24 hours but at the end of the day, if you try to hard and use the conscious mind to master guitar playing, you'll be frustrated. But if you relax and simply practice the lessons you pick up without rushing yourself, you are in effect programming your subconscious mind and with enough practice, your subconscious minds picks up the new target and automatically acquires it. At this point, it becomes mastery and natural.

Now the decision is yours: do you want to reprogram your subconscious mind so that you will genuinely become a natural person and be able to naturally and in due time, consistently manifest high-status body language and naturally attract and seduce beautiful women for your carnal pleasures? If so, then consider the following "codes" you'll need to program into your subconscious mind when it comes to becoming a truly confident Holmes!

Excellence

One mindset that can cause your self-confidence juices to consistently leak and dissipate is that you have to be perfect to be confident in your self and in your manhood. If you think that way, I don't blame you, Dawg! A lot of it has to do with parental issues, e.g., growing up with parents who will only be satisfied with grades less than 100%. Without your consent, your parents or the environment you grew up in (it may be your school) programmed your subconscious mind to acquire perfection as its target.

The problem with perfection as a target is that you can never hit it. Nobody's perfect, bro! And nobody includes you! And if you constantly strive to achieve something that's impossible to achieve, you'll consistently be disappointed or worse, burn out. Either way, that would be a big blow to your self-confidence. And if you're not able to process such failures well, you run the risk of unconsciously programming your conscious mind to accept a new target: failure. Once your subconscious mind accepts its new mission, you'll be powerless (consciously of course) to stop it from making you act like a failure, which will plummet your self-confidence over time.

If you don't believe that there's a way in hell that you can be perfect, just take a look at 2 of the greatest athletes and one of the most successful entrepreneurs in the history of mankind: Michael Jordan, Muhammad Ali and Steve Jobs. If you don't know these homies, then you be alien, dawg!

Let's look at Michael Jordan first – basketball's GOAT or greatest of all time. His career shot percentage – how much of his shots actually went in the basket – is considered to be astounding at 49.7%. What does that tell you? He actually misses slightly more shots than he makes. Is that perfection? Nah! But take a look at the confidence and swagger of the man – legendary!

Let's look at another GOAT, this time for boxing. Muhammad Ali wasn't exactly known for being a humble boxer like Manny Pacquiao – he was sure as hell very confident. But what is his career boxing record? In his 61 professional career fights, he won 56 fights and lost 5. Having lost close to 10% of his fights, can you say he's perfect? Nah...but he the GOAT of boxing, dawg! And he sure ain't shy or bashful!

Lastly, let's take a look at Steve Jobs. Yeah, he a billionaire fo' shuh and he practically revolutionized the way people communicate by creating and popularizing smart phones and tablets. But y'all know after founding Apple, he was booted out? Yeah, Boi – his own company kicked him in the butt out of office. But you know too that he was just so good to be kept out and eventually, he was invited back into it and the rest y'all know is ancient history. Does that sound perfect to you? Nah. But is Steve Jobs' life and accomplishment something you can be proud of if you in his Nikes? Certainly, badass!

So if perfection shouldn't be – and can't be – a goal, what should be? Does it mean I can be a confident sloppy fool? Nah, don't go down the extreme end of the road, bro. The realistic goal you should strive for is excellence. Being confident means being excellent at something...anything! Best is if it's something related to how you and others will see yourself like a job or social skills.

Excellence is being really, really good at something and not being perfect.

Elasticity

When I say elasticity, I don't mean your ability to reach for the girl you fancy from across the room simply by extending your hand to her like Dr. Reed Richards of the Fantastic Four. And for good measure, I'm also not referring to your ability to do the same with your dick-a-doodle-doo. It means that your personality, character and success rate in life aren't fixed – you have the ability to change them.

One of the silliest – and funniest if I may add – mindsets people have is that it's fate that controls their lives and "destinies". Statements like:

"This is how God made me so this is who I'll be forever."

"I come from a poor family. I'll probably die in one too."

"Once shy, always shy."

"I've always failed in my major endeavors. I think it's my fate to be a failure."

Statements like these are some of the most confidence-hostile mindsets one can ever have. Why? It's because confidence is anchored in either actual success or hope for future ones and these kinds of statements both lack acknowledgement of actual success – however small they may be – and hope for future success.

While it's true that there are many things beyond your control, there are many important ones that are within your circle of influence. You need to believe that your mind, personality and current status isn't permanent and that you have the power to change them. Once you do, true confidence will start to stem from within and outward.

The Confidence-Achievement-Confidence Spiral

While it's absolutely true that true confidence stems mostly from actual achievements, it doesn't have to start from there. If that were the case, then how about those who have no meaningful achievements to boast of? How can they become truly confident and win the ladies over? Are they doomed to fail and live a life of compulsory celibacy? I empathically express my objection to such!

So how should you deal with this conundrum? If you're one of those really unfortunate people who have no achievements to start building your confidence on, then you can start building that foundation by acting and thinking confident.

I never said they don't work.

I just said you can't enjoy a solid and long-lasting self-confidence if all you had were acting and thinking confident with no meaningful successes or achievements tucked under your belt.

When you program your unconscious to believe that you can build long-lasting solid self-confidence even without meaningful achievements to begin with, you'll be open to – excited even – to employ the following self-confidence quick hits to give your sagging confidence just enough boost to help you start collecting small victories that will eventually snowball into bigger and meaningful ones.

DELETING THE OLD PROGRAMS OR CODES

Now that you know some of the important programs or codes that should be inputted in your subconscious mind, it's time to make room in your unconscious hard drive for them. And now, my friend, we'll need to delete some of those old and outmoded files with the effective Version 2.0 ones we talked about.

There are several ways to do this, with each technique varying in ease and cost. Let's now look at some of these practical ways of deleting the old programs and codes that are keeping your Alpha Lion all caged up. Let's start uprooting self-confidence debilitating mindsets to make room for new ones.

Hang Out With The Alphas

There's a saying that birds of the same feathers flock together. Maybe it's because great minds think alike! While it means that dawgs of the same kind have the tendency to be drawn to each other, I believe you can use this in a different spin: hang out with those who you want to become in order to be influenced into becoming like them.

When I was a kid, I hung out with the middle pack – those who were neither cool nor uncool. We the average people, man. I realized hanging out with average people also made me, well, average. That changed when I hung out with people who were confident and popular. As I hung out more and more with them, it somehow helped build my self-confidence enough to take on bigger goals and achieve them. If I hadn't hung out with them, my old mindset of "average" and "lack of confidence" wouldn't have been uprooted.

Hanging out with an alpha pack also gives you the benefit of learning from experience in two ways. First, you learn through other alpha males' experiences – particularly what works and what doesn't – so you don't have to commit the same mistake yourself. Second, as you learn from them, you can start applying them in your life with the benefit of being guided and mentored by these uber-confident guys. As you continue learning from experience, you'll be able to delete your old and outdated codes and programs to make room for the newer and more updated ones.

Question Thyself

Another way to delete old programs and codes is by challenging them. As with most dictators and authoritarians, they ability to stay in power and control lives were highly dependent on breaking the wills of their constituents or slaves. Their downfall started and came to pass when more and more people challenged the status quo.

It's the same with your old mindsets or programs/codes. You chip away at them as you challenge them by asking questions that will cast doubt as to their validity and relevance in your life. Actually, you're probably doing that already when you question your ability to be confident. Why not work it the other way around?

I want you to imagine a scene from your favorite law-themed movie or TV series like The Client or Law And Order. How do defense attorneys – those who defend the accused criminals – establish the innocence of their clients? By establishing reasonable doubt about the validity of the evidences presented. And how do they do that? By asking questions.

You can do the same about your existing outdated and impotent self-confidence codes. Let's use the example of the skewed perception that confidence is about being insensitive. Ask yourself: Why do I equate self-confidence with being insensitive to other people? Question every answer until you see why the belief that being self-confident will make you an insensitive person that will most likely drive away women than attract them. Some of the questions you can ask yourself regarding your old, outdated codes and programs (wrong mindsets) are:

"How much of this is true? Is it true at all? Why is it that many of the most confident alpha males that are very good with women that I know of like James Bond aren't insensitive or rude to others?"

"Is this belief beneficial for me or not? Will ditching this belief be beneficial for me or will it just harm me? Will I be able to be as good as with the ladies as James Bond if I continue holding on to this belief?"

Don't Feed The Beast

One of the best ways to successfully beat a formidable adversary is to let it die of hunger. Sure, it may take a longer time than simply delivering a swift blow to the head but it is very effective. No one ever lived without eating, right? Contrast it to boxers and mixed martial arts fighters, most of whom are still around to fight after being hit in the head with many swift blows to the noggin'. Your old programs or codes, a.k.a., mindsets are like fighters: often times, swift blows to the head aren't enough to maim or kill them but depriving them of food long enough will surely lead to death.

To understand how you can starve your old mindsets to death, you need to first understand how you're feeding them. One of the most common but unconscious ways you do it is by meditating on it – and by that I don't mean wearing tights and contorting your body in many different ways that aren't nowhere near sexy while chanting stuff like "ohm" or "shuhmmm". Meditation simply means thinking about something over and over and over, like when you fantasize about all the great sex positions you'll do with Scarlett Johansson or Megan Fox while romanticizing your hand. Yeah, Boi, that's what I'm talking about.

But seriously, if you constantly think about how difficult it would be for you to successfully and consistently employ high status body language and successfully screw women, that's your meditation. And that way, you feed the beast!

So how do you starve it? Simple – stop thinking about it! Whenever it pops into your head, simply acknowledge it and then let it go. Refuse to do more than acknowledge, which you'll need to do because if you deny it, you won't be able to kill it. Let it go by thinking about your new self-confidence programs or codes.

Remember, the more you starve your mindset beast, the more you weaken it until it dies.

What you resist, persists. What you accept, it goes away.

Reprogramming Your Mind For Badass Confidence

"Your mind is a garden. Your thoughts are the seeds. You can grow flowers or you can grow weeds." – Ritu Ghatourey

Now that you've deleted your outdated and harmful self-confidence programs or codes, it's time to install updated and appropriate ones. So how do you do it? This is what this chapter's about, dawg!

AFFIRMATIONS

One of the greatest tennis players of all time once said: use it or lose it. Jimmy Connors may not have been aware of it but what he said wasn't just limited to tennis playing skills – it's applicable to practically any skill or competency.

When it comes to your thoughts, you can think of it as like a skill or a muscle. Using the analogy of muscles, stroke victims – particularly those who suffer from massive ones – usually lose the ability to move or use certain muscles, whether temporarily or permanently. Temporary loss of use of muscles is often due to not being able to use them for an extended period of time. And why is lack of use detrimental to them? It's because it makes muscles shrink, also known as atrophy. When muscles atrophy, it's not just muscle mass that's reduced. The ability to use them and their strength are reduced too.

Your mind is the same. If you don't use it often or as hard, it atrophies. Your mental agility and ability to control your thoughts and shape your attitudes diminish, making you more susceptible to being affected by external factors. In other words, you become more and more powerless to influence your life, including your ability to be truly confident about yourself.

Positive affirmations or positive self-talk, as it's more popularly known, is one of the best ways to exercise your mind muscle in order to beef up your self-confidence. It's one of the best ways to reprogram your subconscious mind into acquiring a new and much better target: a truly confident you. So use it or lose it, bro!

How does using positive affirmations look like in real, practical life? The first step is to take a piece of paper, preferably an A4-sized typing paper and fold it in 2 lengthwise. Write all the wrong mindsets you have about being a truly self-confident dude on the left side and as you do it, don't limit yourself to what I wrote earlier – feel free to add more that you feel are keeping you from becoming truly confident.

When you're done, write all the new mindsets or up-to-date self-confidence programs or codes that you'd want to replace the wrong, outdated ones with on the right side. When you're done, tear the paper in half along the fold and destroy the side that contains the wrong, outdated self-confidence mindsets and programs. Make as many copies as you can of the remaining list and post copies of it in all rooms or areas of your house so you'll be able to read them aloud as often and as much as you like – self-talk. It may not look like much in terms of helping you score chicks, but believe me, it will help you lots by helping you feel truly confident about yourself. When you're confident, your high status body language will look all the more natural and suave.

What if you've already reached the point where you've already installed your up-to-date and helpful programs or codes in your subconscious mind? Does it mean you should stop talking yourself confident? I empathically object to such a horrendous thought, dude! Why? It's because better to err on the side of caution. By continuing to do so, you continue to strengthen the new mindsets you already have and minimize the risk of any unwanted external influence or program from subtly trickling into your already confident subconscious mind. Remember, successful mutinies start out subtle and small. Give no room for the enemy to reclaim your mind, my friend!

HANGING OUT WITH THE ALPHAS

Surprise, surprise! This one makes a comeback. As I've indirectly mentioned earlier about deleting outdated self-confidence programs and codes (mindsets), hanging out with the kinds of people you want to be – confident alpha males – also helps you install updated and appropriate self-confidence programs and codes effortlessly.

It's like trying to get a tan. You don't have to exert a lot of effort – you simply expose yourself to the sun. In this case, you expose yourself to the awesomeness and oozing self-confidence of alpha males.

There's a saying that more is caught than taught. It means you learn more by observing and trying than studying. By hanging out with alpha males, you'll eventually catch their confidence without trying hard and you'll be able to naturally and effortlessly exhibit high status body language for scoring all the chicks you want, Dawg! I may repeat it over and over again, because this factor is really paramount for your future success with women and life.

JUST DO IT

Remember what I discussed about the Confidence- Achievement- Confidence Spiral earlier? Practicing or living out your new programs or mindsets is one of the best ways to really hammer it into your subconscious mind. I remember when I first applied a technique to get women's phone numbers. Unconsciously, I didn't believe it yet. I just used my conscious mind to give it my best try. My first time at applying that technique was successful. I got the woman's number, which to me was a major victory akin to winning World Wars I and II! That experience helped convince my subconscious mind that it's a program worth installing in my mental hard drive. By simply acting confident through application of what I learned, I was able to achieve small successes that helped build up my self-confidence that allowed me to take bigger and bolder actions that eventually led to many unforgettable banging experiences, bro!

Now that we've laid the foundations for your badass high status body language, let the games begin!

Robert Moore

The 10 Principles of High Status Body Language

Now I will show you different high status body language positions and principles.

First of all, understand that as a high status man, you will always make yourself comfortable first, wherever you go. That's not a selfish behavior, since it will give everyone else around you the permission to relax, feel good and be comfortable too.

#1 principle: take up more space.

Low status people tend to make themselves small, invisible, sitting or standing in an uncomfortable way. They are not sending their energy out to the world, because they don't see themselves as high status persons: in their mind they're not worth it.

They're closed on themselves; they're hiding from the outside world.

You, on the other hand, will think that your energy is so valuable that of course you're willing to share it with the world, so you're going to open yourself and take up more space.

Spread your legs and your arms: be comfortable!

You may ask, why is that so? It's because shy and unconfident people are more concerned about what people will say. They're too afraid of "offending" people or getting really bad comments about them like they're insensitive, arrogant or being chutzpah-tic.

And if you were paying attention, you'll remember that these are the 3 common misconceptions about confidence that turn most men off from even the idea of becoming confident. This is a potent disease called "people pleasing".

Confident, alpha men aren't concerned with people's opinions and comments because they're sure of themselves. They do respect other people's opinions and beliefs and as such, they also respect their own. They're also able to draw a fine line between respect and pleasing.

Many people feel it isn't right to take up more than the usual personal space. Take note, it's a relative term and not an absolute, moral issue. So take up as much space as you want. Just don't overdo it and crossover from being a confident sexy alpha stud to an obnoxious son of a whore. There's a big difference.

Standing over a table with your palms flat on the table and arms wide, leaning in forward a bit is a great power pose. Sitting back and opening your arms, folding your hands behind your head is another one. Sitting with wide legs and open arms is another still. Standing with your legs slightly wider than your hips and your hands on your hips with your arms out at your sides is known as "the superman" power pose.

These wide, open and confident poses have actually been proven to stimulate the production of testosterone in both males and females. Testosterone helps to reduce cortisol and increase serotonin production – the "happy hormone". It also adds to a boost of confidence.

Experiments have been done by having people practice these power poses for two minutes before taking mock job interviews that they were unaware of being staged. Another group was asked to hold a closed off, insecure pose for 2 minutes before such an interview.

From the results of the interviews, it was observed that the people who held insecure poses were not any less-qualified candidates for the job, but they were remarked as being less appealing candidates because of their quiet or withdrawn manner.

The people who had held power poses two minutes before the interview were noted as being engaging, confident, a pleasure to talk to, as well as interesting and appealing enough to be asked in for a second interview or be offered a job.

So when it comes to figuring out how you are used to carrying yourself, use the body awareness you've developed and simply ask yourself: "am I closed or open right now?"

You'll know the answer: take action and open up the positioning of your body.

#2 principle: show your crotch.

Dominant men who attract, seduce and fu*k a lot of girls, have no problem showing their sexuality to the world.

So, don't be afraid to draw attention to the crotch region of your body while you're sitting. Open your legs, maybe put a hand in that region to subconsciously draw attention there; showing a nice belt can help you, too.

Aren't your proud of who you are?

Aren't you proud of your body and your incredibly energetic, attractive sex drive?

Always show your pride: be a MAN, be proud of your sexuality.

Now don't get the wrong idea here. There's a difference between teasing and being Hervert The Pervert.

Teasing is confidently sexy. Hervert The Pervert isn't. For one, don't do this and wear really tight fitting pants that bulge your manliness. That's more of a symptom of an exhibitionist sex maniac than a smooth, confidently suave George Clooney.

Another thing you shouldn't do to look more like Hervert than George is don't obviously point to your cock and worse, look at her with a devilish smile and grin. Again, you'll look more like a stalker than anything.

And of course you don't need to have the length and girth of Jack Napier or Mandingo to confidently expose your crotch region. Remember, self-confidence! A big cock won't do much with miniscule confidence.

Just ask Napoleon Bonaparte.

#3 principle: slow down your movements.

Move slower!

Low status people move quickly and fidgety, they're not comfortable, they don't believe in themselves.

From now on, you'll cut your movements in half.

When you're walking, when you're turning your head, whenever you're moving your body around, do it slower, in half the time you do it right now.

Why do you need to take it slow? A big part of being confident is knowing that you're doing things at your own terms: your time, your way, and your call.

So how do you normally do things when you know you're not pressured by deadlines or you have all the time in the world? That's right – you're not in an effin' hurry! You take your sweet time. You're relaxed.

When you're not in control, guess what – someone or something else is!

When that happens, you don't call the shots and often times, you're hurrying things up because you're dancing to other people's music. You almost always don't have as much time as you'd like to finish your assignment or responsibility. And when you don't have much control over your life, your confidence plummets. And moving very quickly all the time sends the vibe that you're not in control. And that's not confident or sexy.

Another reason why confident alpha males move slower than the omega men is because they're very competent, in bed or otherwise. By taking their time, they show women that they have the ability to get things done well and on time – again, a control issue.

The first reason for moving slow is all about showing authority over one's self and the other is about authority over others, be it people or circumstances, as manifested by results.

Moreover, moving slower and speaking intentionally slower gives you more time to think about your exact actions and words with what you want to say. The more accurate and concise you can be with your actions and words, the more steadfast you appear to others. You'll also feel more confident with yourself and what your own desires and beliefs are.

Moving and speaking slower also helps you to get the bottom of what your true desires are so that you can bring those into the world and share them with others.

As the saying goes, "Think fast and speak slowly".

So take it slower, badass!

#4 principle: be non-reactive.

Don't react to something outside of your reality. When you're talking with a girl and you hear a siren or a noise, do not turn your head. Stay focused on her and she will feel your masculine, dominant power. She won't look at the source of the noise and she will stay in the moment, following your high status behavior.

Often being *reactive* in a situation can lead to further trouble or complications.

On the other hand, being *responsive* means that you remain grounded in your central sense of conviction for yourself and your confidence. You may feel emotions triggered within you due to some situation, but you allow them to pass through you or channel them in some other way rather than get carried away by them in thought, verbal or physical reaction.

When you're responsive, you take your time to reply to a situation or stimulus mindfully and appropriately. You develop an ability to handle situations with ease, command, and a sense of humor.

Also, be aware of your fidgety movements and correct them: maybe while you're talking to her, you're also touching your hands, or you're moving your feet as a sign of anxiety.

Stop doing that. Be still and relaxed.

With all due respect to women, being a very reactive person is so girly. Nothing else screams "girly man" than being reactive. So why does being reactive scream to a hot woman that you're more feminine than her?

I'd like you to think of a time when most things, if not everything in your life was going as planned. How'd you feel?

You probably felt great, steady, calm or at peace. In short, you feel really confident. When one or two curve balls come your way, you're too peaceful to react inappropriately. You react in a calm and collected manner because you know that in the grander scheme of things, you're in control of your life and one or two mishaps won't change that fact.

Now think of a time when most things, if not everything in your life wasn't going your way. How did you feel? Among many other things, I bet you felt you have no control over your life and your situation, which made you high-strung too.

Being reactive to things and people sends the subtle signal to woman that you're highly-strung. Being highly-strung means you feel you generally have little or no control over your life, much less the situation you're in. And that feeling will be strongly transmitted to each and every woman you are planning to score with, which will of course turn them off leaving you as celibate as the Pope.

Try not to be reactive. If you're not yet that confident, don't worry. You can control your impulses and if you do that long and often enough, you'll be able to reprogram your subconscious mind that you really are confident and non-reactive, which will enable you to unconsciously and naturally act that way all the time.

#5 principle: lean back.

Learn to lean back most of the time.

Remember that leaning in is a really low status behavior. Learn to make people, especially girls, feel a subconscious urge to lean towards you, simply by leaning back.

This little trick will change the whole dynamic of your conversations, giving you the power of a badass.

This also means that when you're walking or just standing, you will have your shoulders up and back and your chin up. Just a masculine, healthy posture.

Look at this picture: who is perceived as the highest status person here?

Berlusconi is relaxed, he's leaning back and his legs are crossed.

Obama is leaning forward, his hands are closed, as well as his legs.

The answer is clear, right? This time, the Italian wins.

Think of it this way, leaning forward or backward communicates two opposite sentiments. Leaning forward is a sign of interest – maybe too much of it.

When you're too interested in others, it sends the signal that you don't find yourself interesting enough, that you're following rather than leading, or like in this picture, you accede that the other person is superior to you.

Leaning backward sends different messages to a woman and other people about how you feel about yourself and others. One is that you're of course, confident. Why? It's because leaning back means you're relaxed and believe me badass, only people who are truly relaxed can afford to lean back and hold that position long enough.

Those who aren't confident will find this to be a very awkward position and after a minute or two, they'll revert to their original and consistent omega male, low status posture.

Second, leaning back sends the message that you're not that interested in the hot chick you're with or eyeing. Believe it or not, this can pose a very big challenge for hot women who are used to being pursued, hounded and served by omega men.

They're used to "controlling" men that when they find you're not that interested and aren't willing to interact on her terms of dominance, they'll sense deep inside that you're no ordinary man – you're alpha! And when that happens, consider her leaving the front door to her pants open for you!

Lastly, leaning back tells the world that you sincerely believe you're worthy to be followed – that they should follow you. That tells a lot about your confidence level and your ability to control yourself and your situation.

So lean back, relax and enjoy.

If you're talking to a girl in a loud club (or whatever loud place) then move slowly, lean in, whisper your words into her ear and then go back to leaning back. This will make her come to you whispering in your ear: that's how high status men communicate in loud places, without leaning in as a low status guy.

#6 principle: lean against things whenever you can.

Have you ever seen a picture of James Dean?

When you're talking next to a wall, lean against it. Just like James Dean did, always remembering that showing your crotch region is important.

Also, having a wall behind you and a room in front of you is a high status position. You're in control of the situation in front of you and, subconsciously, you will be recognized as the leader of your group.

Leaning against a wall also sends the message that you're relaxed, calm and collected. These further imply that things are going according to your plans and that you're in control of yourself and your situations. And you know what that means, Dawg. If you don't, then here it is: you're subtly telling a woman that you're so in control that she can't order you around and that she's gonna have to play by your own rules.

That should make you stand out in her mind as not being an ordinary mortal but that you're different from all the other wimpy omega males surrounding her and vying for her attention. And that should also open her front door into her pants later on.

#7 principle: strong eye contact.

A high status male will make strong, powerful eye contact when he's talking to a girl, but he will make less eye contact when she's talking to him.

This will make her work harder to gain his attention and win his approval.

That's called the *90/60 Rule*. If you want to know more about this powerful attraction technique, check out my other book *"Eye Contact Training"*.

You can find it here: http://amzn.to/1MtxaiN

That simple trick will subconsciously communicate more high status in just a few seconds. But how's that so?

It's been said that there are only 2 kinds of people who can't look at others in the eyes: one who's hiding a lie and one who's hiding love or attraction. Although the last one seems more "adorable", it isn't sexy. In fact, both aren't sexy because hiding something means fear and lack of confidence. And that my dear friend, ain't sexy at all.

Do you remember when you were a kid and you did something you know will definitely tick your folks off? When you were trying to hide it, were you able to talk to them normally by looking them in the eye? I bet your answer is "no". Now do you see how eye contact communicates high status – or lack thereof – in so short a time?

So do yourself a favor and next time you talk to people, especially hot women, establish strong eye contact: let them know who's in control of the situation!

#8 principle: no fake laugh.

Imagine a group of employees sitting at a table with their boss. He makes a bad joke but since everyone there recognize him as the higher status person, they will feel they HAVE to laugh.

Keep in mind that you should laugh when you're out with people and friends, of course!

The general rule I'm giving you here is this: if you truly think something is funny, then fu*king laugh; but if something isn't funny, DO NOT fake laugh.

Faking your laugh isn't something that's hard to figure out, like say, a quadratic or a stochastic calculus equation. To the contrary, it's as easy to figure out as whether or not Jennifer Lopez is wearing panties beneath the gowns that she wears in major showbiz awards nights. Yeah Boi, it's that easy!

But it's not the ease by which people can tell if you're faking a laugh or not that matters here – it's what it says about you. Faking your laugh is one of the biggest "I'm a certified, licensed and chartered people pleaser" signs you can post on your forehead.

It simply shows you're that eager to please or avoid offending people that you're willing to not be yourself – it's as if the real you isn't admirable or acceptable. Once that hot women pick up on that, it's time to say hello to a vow of celibacy!

From now on, banish from your life all of your fake smiles and fake laughs.

Cut them out entirely.

#9 principle: wide animation of presentation.

Move your hands! Don't be afraid to use your arms and facial expressions to emote and express your feelings while you're talking.

Be comfortable sharing all your emotions with the world.

Keep everything smooth and controlled, don't go too big or try hard.

Only the former comes off as high status.

Why is this a high status gesture? Why, oh why Delilah?

Consider the last time you were so into something or someone. How did you feel at that time? I bet you felt positively strong about it or that person. Your excitement or appreciation of that thing or person was probably very obvious to your friends or family that without a doubt, they knew you were telling the truth. They felt your passion about what your talking about.

Women – and even men – find passion to be a very sexy and attractive personal quality or characteristic. Why? Because being passionate about something or someone shows that you don't care about what people may think about you. People who are passionate about music don't care if people think they're poor – they love music and as long as they don't step on other people's toes, they stick to their guns!

And what does such lack of care for what others think communicate? That's right, badass – confidence! Passion equals strong confidence in what you're doing and who you are as a person. And such confidence is so high status sexy.

#10 principle: keep the tension.

Be okay with blinking less. Pierce a girl's soul just by looking in her eyes.

A strong eye contact builds tension. When there's tension in a situation, the person who's more comfortable with that tension is ALWAYS the higher status one.

Tension, at the right amount and kind, is a high status move to lure the ladies in and get in their pants because it generates so much excitement. But why is excitement such a big deal if you want to seduce her into taking off her panties for ya?

Consider the fact that beautiful and hot women are so used to being the boss. Men surround her like moth to a flame and since most men don't have a clue as to how attraction works in women, they tend to win her over by showering her with gifts, affection, favors and what-nots. In other words, most men try to win her over by spoiling her – granter her every wish and whim, whenever possible.

But there's a very big problem with that – having too much of a good thing too easy all the time often leads to boredom or worse, contempt. Boredom because you are very predictable and contempt because you're just adding to her boredom and irritation with all the other men. By trying to please her all the time, you don't set yourself apart from all the other omega wussies that have been surrounding and hounding her since time immemorial.

Creating the right kind and amount of tension, however, will set you apart in 2 ways.

First, you're different. You make it quite uncomfortable for her, which is a sensation she probably hasn't felt in quite a long while.

Second, you make her guess what's coming up next. Tension is often due to uncertainty as to what will happen next. By being different and unpredictable, you create excitement in her. And excitement trumps boredom anytime, anywhere.

Excitement invigorates her, especially if she hasn't felt it from a man in a long while. She be going like "His stare is quite uncomfortable. Is he attracted to me or is he just like that? Most men don't look at me that way so it must be that he's attracted to me. But it can also be he's like that to all women he talks to. What's the deal. Dammit...I don't know what to make of this...it excites me!"

And that my dear friend, is why creating tension is such a high status technique that you should include in your high status body language arsenal.

That's why I dedicated a whole book on mastering eye contact.

Again, as I told you before, if you want to know more about it, you can find it searching Eye Contact Training on Amazon.com.

Be comfortable with that tension and blink less often. Keep the tension both with your eyes and with your body: remember to move slowly, don't rush your movements.

So, let's do a quick recap now.

Look at this picture and check the presence of the principles in these two different body language displays.

Hey! I have no political interests here.

I just want you to be a master of body language for the rest of your life.

So who in this picture is perceived as the highest status individual, in your opinion?

As you may notice, the answer is Vladimir Putin.

Look at his feet: they are grounded, strong and commanding. He proudly shows his crotch, his legs are open and his shoulders are back, wide and relaxed.

On the other side, look at Obama.

His feet are not grounded, they're backtracking and weak, because they're standing on their toes. His legs are not that open, he's hiding his crotch. His shoulders are not relaxed and wide: they're closed and he's leaning forward. He's even hiding his lips!

In just one picture, you can find the results of the application of so many principles and traits.

Look at it one more time and save it in your subconscious: it'll be helpful for every social interaction!

Robert Moore

Tips and Tricks for a Dominant Body Language

There are some little tricks you can implement in your daily behavior that will make you more powerful in your conversations, especially with girls.

#1 trick: always leave the conversation first.

When you're talking to a girl, don't wait for her to leave the conversation: the first person leaving it is generally perceived as the higher status one. Why is that so, badass?

The generally polite, a.k.a., people pleasing way of ending a conversation is to wait for others to end it for you, e.g., the other person ends it first or circumstances like a fire or an earthquake disrupts it enough as to end it.

There's nothing wrong with being polite or a people pleaser per se. But if you're trying to seduce and attract the ladies in the house, everything's wrong with both.

Robert Moore

Women are drawn – attracted to men who are in control of themselves, their situations and the women themselves. By trying to please people, you show that you're not in control and that you're not confident in yourself that you need others' approval. And because waiting for the other party to end the conversation every time wreaks of people pleasing, it's a subtle way of telling women that you're not confident and you're not in control, even of such a minor thing as a conversation.

That's why ending conversations first is so high status, badass. You subtly but effectively tell the other person – and that woman you've been wanting to shag – who's in control. And that's no other than you, because you're going down your path, you're on a mission!

I suggest you watch at least the first episode of the first season of Suits, the TV show. Watch how non-reactive, dominant, badass Harvey Specter is. Watch closely how he always ends conversations first, by leaving his interlocutor, who of course is charmed and can't even respond to such a high level of badassery.

There is another simple way to look willing to leave: if you want to give her the FEELING that you can leave at every moment, then you can use the foot trick.

The direction where your feet are pointed at indicates where your interest is.

So, if they are both pointed directly at the girl you're talking with, it is a clear sign of interest in keeping the conversation going.

In order to make her work harder for your attention, try to turn a feet outward.

It's so subconscious but she will perceive you as more valuable and she'll start fighting for your attention.

Try that and thank me later, badass.

#2 trick: high status seated positions.

If you want a powerful seated position, then try this: legs crossed, crotch out, arms taking up space on the back of your seat.

Another way is legs open, crotch in sight, drawing attention to that region, and arms taking up space.

The key principle is: *wherever you go, you make yourself comfortable first and you take up your personal space.*

If there aren't comfortable spots in your room, make yourself as comfortable as you can in that situation and then, when you have the opportunity, take your space immediately. Don't hesitate!

In case you weren't paying attention earlier, Holmes, taking up more space is one way of subtly sending the message to everyone that you're confident, in control and in charge. This is the principle behind a high status sitting position. The position, postures and gestures I mentioned are all about sending that message through personal space.

Claiming space is one way of showing superiority and supremacy, just don't be a bully like China, who occupies space despite the legitimate diplomatic protests of many weaker nations. Remember, true superiority and supremacy isn't the same as bullying people. Keep that in mind.

And make sure that the chair you're sitting in is sturdy or stable enough to hold your weight as you execute this trick. If it breaks down and your cheeks – butt ones – kiss the floor, there goes your aura of confidence, superiority and supremacy. Ladies and gentlemen, high status just left the building – in a hurry!

#3 trick: be confident with your thumbs.

Every great leader out there knows that your thumbs are the most confident of your fingers.

Hands in the pockets, focus on your thumb: you can either choose thumb out and fingers in, or thumb in and fingers out. They are both high status positions.

NEVER hands completely in the pockets: that's the lowest status position.

#4 trick: arms crossed

That's not necessarily a bad thing: if you're talking to a girl and she wants to earn your attention and win your approval, then you can stand straight, powerful, with your chin up and arms crossed.

This position says: "Ok, you're funny! Try to earn my attention, show me what you got".

Normally, a crossed-arm posture isn't a desirable one when it comes to general interpersonal communications. But if you're trying to seduce women and get her to take her clothes off, you need veer off the tried and tested safe road of general interpersonal communications skills. In fact, you'll need to do many things that contradict the general communication principles of being open, courteous and nice because in doing so, you can create the tension levels necessary to push her attraction buttons effectively.

Robert Moore

Think of it this way – hot and beautiful women are generally overexposed to bashful, courteous and polite omega males. Chances are, they're craving for more excitement from the men they come into contact with. If you want to set yourself apart from the multitudes of omega wussies that normally come her way, you'll need to create excitement and as I discussed earlier, tension is one of the best ways to create that!

Because crossed-arms are usually thought of as not compliant with social graces and people pleasing during conversations, doing so while talking to a beautiful woman may make her a bit uncomfortable – creating some tension. But that's good tension because it's the kind of tension that doesn't bully or disrespect her but at the same time tells her you're not the boss of me. It's that tension that will get her to wonder "Is he just lacking in social, people pleasing graces or he just doesn't care about what I think of him? The nerve...but I think I like it. Dammit...why am I feeling this way? I'm confused...and excited! He's different from all the others."

And that, badass, is why crossing your arms is a high status attraction technique!

#5 trick: manage critiques.

If you claim your high status and start displaying a powerful, dominant body language, then some people may become jealous.

Don't worry: they're just projecting their insecurities and fears onto you. Don't fight it, accept it and go back to your high status.

Ignore their mediocrity.

Doing so is a great attraction builder because it shows you're that secure with yourself and that you're not affected by your critics. Remember how being non-reactive is a high status technique that attracts women because it shows you're that confident in your self, your abilities and in your track record? That's the main principle here.

By not fighting your critics, you're essentially saying that you're so secure with yourself that none of your criticisms matter enough to be worthy of your time and attention – that you have more important things to do in your life. By accepting it without any admission of guilt or denying of such, you send an even more powerfully confident message: that you respect others' contrary opinions and that you're just that secure with yourself to be able to do so.

Now that is what I call class. And class is very high status, badass!

#6 trick: don't be afraid to claim your high status.

If you're afraid to do it, banish that part of you from your life. Fear can be a very subtle but powerful agent that can sabotage your high status efforts by slowly eating at your core like termites do to wooden foundations of houses. Over time, it can cause all your high status efforts to come crashing down if you don't keep it in check.

Remember this:

Everyone wants YOU to be high status.

They always had, even if they couldn't say it.

It makes everyone who hangs around with you feel better and cooler.

Just like you want to hang out with cool, powerful people, your friends want the same.

They want YOU to be high status: maybe after a couple weeks, when they had accepted your change... but they will for sure.

The Badass Body Language Training

Now that you know about the key principles of a powerful body language, it's time to TRAIN it.

You goal is to constantly show a dominant body language without even thinking about it, in every situation.

So, the #1 way to train it is to *make constant practice all the time.*

Wherever you are, maybe at work, at gym, at home, be aware of how you're sitting or how you're standing. In a couple of weeks it will become really natural, but start with the awareness first.

I'm gonna give it to you straight, that at first, it ain't gonna be easy or natural. Remember, if you're reading this book, it means you're not yet there! You haven't mastered the art of the high status body language yet and have still to achieve your desired sex life, eh? I thought so. As such, it's gonna take much effort, process and deliberation at first.

Consider a piece of prime real estate that's located in a spot that you really, really love. It's a spot that you intensely desire to have at all costs. That's where you want to build your dream home. The only challenge is that there's an existing structure on that lot. What's a badass like you to do?

First, you'll have to demolish the old structure and doing so takes time and accuracy. Sure, you can just plant several C4 explosives and blow the structure to smithereens. There's a problem with that quick approach though.

First, it's gonna get you in trouble with the law. It's simply illegal. Second, assuming that it is legal to do that, simply blowing up the structure won't make it ideal or even fit to build your dream home on. You'll have to precisely remove all those debris and old foundations to make way for a new one upon which your new home will be built. It takes time, effort and deliberate action – just like with our body language training.

As you practice the things you learned here, the first part is demolishing the old "structures" in your head, which is your unconscious behavior. And to do that, you'll need to pay really close attention to how you act around people, especially hot girls, within the first few days or weeks probably. As you continue consciously utilizing the principles, you'll find that the structure will eventually be demolished and that you're starting to lay the foundations and soon, be acting them out naturally.

Part of the conscious demolishing and re-building is self-correction. This can only work if you put in the effort to really be conscious or mindful of your practicing the principles. Constantly self-correct: if you find yourself seated in a low status positions, just recognize it and correct yourself.

Fix your posture and go back dominating your path.

#2 way: *take one of the ten principles and practice it each day.*

Each day, choose a principle and focus on it: you will find that each of those things will come off naturally and in automatic, very quickly.

So, for example, start focusing on taking up more space. The first day you will share your energy with the world and practice all the positions related to this principle.

The next day, focus on drawing attention on your crotch, open up, show your masculinity to the world. And so on, with all the other principles.

I know it can be really tempting to just go all gung ho and practice or employ all the principles at once, Dawg. I feel ya'! I'm sure that after reading and learning these principles, you're a super eager beaver (hmmm...the beaver analogy doesn't sound right) that wants to master everything as soon as possible and start on your Don Juan of your generation...or neighborhood.

But herein lies the problem with that, my friend. By taking on too many things, you compromise your ability to master each of them. In other words, you may just end up to be a Jack-of-all-trades and a master of none. Worse, you might even fail to become a Jack of any of the 10 principles. Now that would be a shame, eh?

What you need to be like is a light from a magnifying glass that you used to burn holes on a paper with or start a fire. An unfocused light, one that's all over the place is not powerful enough to burn a hole through paper and start a fire. But using a magnifying glass, you hyper focus light into one tight space and concentrate its heat on one tiny spot. Such concentration allows it to burn a hole or start a fire.

Do you remember how you learned to run as a child? Didn't you start off by learning how to sit down first as a baby? Then from that, didn't you learn how to crawl, then stand, then wobble, then walk and eventually run? Why didn't you learn all of it at once? My point exactly.

So do the same when it comes to practicing the principles you learned here. Take one principle at a time and don't rush into the next one. Be focused yet relaxed and don't try to hard because doing so will only make it harder for you to master the principle. Don't focus on one thousand things each day: just pick one and master it.

#3 way: *become a long-term student of body language.*

Although body language can be a relatively fixed area of study in the sense that there are only so many gestures, postures and mannerisms can be used for attracting and seducing women, it doesn't mean you should stop studying it once you feel you've gotten it down to pat.

This book is just the beginning of your life-long internship under the master named High Status Body Language. I'm just one of the many teachers under that Master and as much as like to claim I'm the only one, I can't.

After this, you can buy other books on effective interpersonal (or sexual) communications in order for you to continue successfully drawing the ladies in and having the best times of your life. You can also buy my other nonverbal communication books for further and deeper study, in case you haven't bought them yet. My point is, consider this as a lifetime process of continuous evolution.

Find mentors and follow their advice. Don't envy them, emulate their process!

Consider a Samurai or a Katana sword. Those are some of the sharpest weapons on the face of the earth and can easily decapitate anyone's head, above or below. But for all it's sharpness and durability, did you know that they still require regular sharpening? Yes man, they do.

It's the same with you!

However sharp you eventually become at the art of high status body language for drawing the ladies in, you will eventually get dull doing the same things with the same results over and over again. You may not believe me but at some point, you'll reach a point that you may actually get bored doing the same easy thing over and over again. By continuing to be a student of the craft, you don't just minimize boredom – you also get better and better at it and as a result, be able to take on more challenging women.

How's that for an incentive to continue learning?

Study, watch, notice, observe, be aware of your and other's body language. Notice how high status body language gets attraction and power from girls, coworkers, bosses.

Don't let the *content* of certain situations (what people are saying) distract you. Instead, let it come and go and look at the *context*: notice how a high status body language gets attraction from a girl, or a promotion from a boss, and how a low status guy tend to get no girls and be ignored by his boss.

Learn from it, master it and be better at it.

Pick a good model, someone you see at least a couple times a week.

It can be a friend, a guy you work with, someone at the gym.

Just pick a guy you always thought about something like *"damn, that guy always carries himself really f**king well!"*.

Then, start modeling him: notice how he responds in certain situations and what he's communicating with his body and replicate his behavior.

When you're with a girl and don't know how to act, ask yourself: how would that guy from the gym be sitting right now? How would he stand? How would he *FEEL*?

Your brain is going to know the answer: all you have to do is trust it.

Robert Moore

The High Status Walk

The way you walk is incredibly communicative.

It says so many things about yourself, your life, your state and, of course, your status level.

It communicates exactly how you feel about yourself.

Your walk sets the frame people will interpret everything you'll say and do from. Basically, they see you walking and they ask themselves: *"is he high status or is he low status?"*

Obviously, it's way better to be filtered through a high status frame.

Imagine this: two guys say both the same exact words. The former is a dominant, confident, high status individual; the latter is shy, weak and low status. They say: *"ok, let's go"*. The content is the same, but it'll be perceived in two totally different ways.

Remember that the *context* of the interaction is more important than the *content*!

You should have already noticed that every dominant, badass man in history has had a powerful walk.

Think about political leaders or actors like Brad Pitt, Marlon Brando, Ryan Gosling, or characters like James Bond: they have their OWN high status walk, which women find sexually powerful and men immediately recognize as badass.

They walk in different ways, but there are five characteristics that can be easily found in all their movements.

#1: they walk tall and open, with an alpha male posture.

The shoulders are back, squeezing the muscles between the shoulder blades. The chin is up, they're not looking down at their feet, but directly ahead. The back is straight and neutral.

The hands may be in the pockets, but leaving the thumbs out.

Have you ever noticed how James Bond walks into a room? Or how about someone else who you personally know? Don't you notice that some people walk into a room and seem to just immediately "own" it? They come in and all eyes start to gravitate toward him, even if he's not a famous celebrity. There's something about the walking posture that oozes manliness, confidence and sex appeal.

But more than just the walk, the proper gestures and posture helps in your ability to silently scream "Hey, I'm so confident under my own skin that it hurts!" or that "I own this room, homies!"

That's why high status walking involves other equally important gestures like shoulders drawn back, chin up or level with the floor and your back neutral and straight.

Slouched shoulders or shoulders that are drooped forward indicate several negative connotations about you: you're either feeling depressed, sad, hopeless or shy. Either way, all of these indicate you're not in control of yourself, your situations and chances are, of women as well. Ultimately, what this tells others is that you're not confident and you're someone women can just manipulate like a cutesy little puppy.

If you're chin's pointing downward, as if you're looking at your shoes, you also send the message that you're not confident. Looking down, as with inability to make eye contact, is a sign of feeling inferior to other people. Did you notice that most proud people look straight or up but shy and insecure people look down? Have you ever noticed too that guilty people tend to look down as well? So when you walk (or stand), always be mindful that if always looking down won't just get you into an accident but it will also send the signal to women that you're not attractive, interesting or exciting.

#2: they know where they're going.

High status men have a clear purpose in their lives, and they dominate their path, making each and every step count.

They know exactly where they're going, lead forward by their positive masculine energy. Their walks are direct, strong and solid: they give you the idea that they're not f*cking around.

Why is knowing where you're going that important if you want to be considered a high status male? It all boils down to control – and remember how women are so attracted to men who are able to demonstrate or communicate that they are in control of themselves, their situations and of women?

Here's how it works. Imagine a woman daring you to find her house without the benefit of an address or a GPS device and all she gave you were relatively generic descriptions of her home like it's the only blue house in a street with a fortune telling shop within a 6-block radius. And she said you can do anything you want with her if you're able to find her house. How would you go about driving through the streets within that 6-block radius. Chances are you'd do it in a way that from an outsider seems like you're lost. You won't look confident because you don't know where you're going and that you have very little control on your ability to have sex with her in the next 2 hours.

But say she gives you her exact address and it happens to be just down the street where you actually live. I bet you'd drive like a madman who is so confident in his driving skills – no hesitations and minimal stops to validate your location. Why? You already know where it is – where exactly you're going for that all-important booty call!

See the difference? Knowing where you're going – literally or figuratively – makes you more confident than you would've otherwise been if you had no idea. And confidence is the mark of a high status men, which is key to successfully attracting and seducing women.

Oh, and when you know where you're going with what you're doing, you give women the impression that you're the real deal – that you can most probably satisfy her emotional and carnal needs. Yeah badass!

#3: their walk is smooth and controlled.

Their walk is slower than most, because they follow their own chosen pace. Remember that NOTHING makes a high status man walking at a pace he doesn't want to.

They're leaders, they set the tone: they do not rush! Only fools do, as the song goes.

Rushing your walk, as if you're participating in the Boston Marathon but speed walking, makes your walk rough, jerky and look chaotic. Speed walking other than for exercise communicates you're in a hurry, probably because you forgot to turn of the gas at home, that you're late for a very important sales pitch, that you're trying to please your supervisor by coming to work 30 minutes earlier than your official time or that you're hurrying to smother a girl with gifts and serve her like a slave.

Those, badass, aren't badass at all. Those are signs of a wussy – a man who isn't strong enough to be in control of himself, his circumstances and women in general. And guess what? Wussies aren't high status and aren't attractive at all.

When you slow down your walking speed, you're more relaxed – and that'll show! What does relaxed mean? It means you're not in a hurry because you remembered to turn off the gas before leaving the house, that you're early for a very important and career-boosting sales pitch, that you're not trying to please your supervisor just to suck-up and get promoted (an indication that you don't have what it takes to be legitimately promoted) and that you're not under the control of any woman. What these all mean is that you're in control of yourself, your situation and of women themselves.

And that, badass, is so high status. That's so sexy to women.

#4: their walk is a masculine stroll.

They have a confident, masculine stroll. While they're walking, they fuel their energy with positive thoughts and the body can't help but to follow their mind.

They have that little "knowing grin" on their faces.

Their walk is just dominant and relaxed at the same time.

Any wuss of a man can walk but it takes a certain stroll to make him high status. A kind of stroll that screams "manly man!". And it's the kind of stroll that whispers "warning, hot sexy man coming through" to women.

The masculine stroll, more than just a collection of walking gestures, is more about confidence. A masculine stroll is one that just comes out naturally to high status men because, well, they're confident. It's like asking how birds mastered the art of flying. Well, it's because they're birds! If you're confident, you'll walk high status.

Remember your torpedo missile of an subconscious mind? If your subconscious mind is still programmed or coded to acquire low status behavior, then you will naturally have more feminine or asexual stroll instead of a masculine one. But if you did your homework and have started to experience some level of success in terms of acquiring a genuine sense of self-confidence, then a masculine stroll will just flow out from you!

Yes, you can fake it but whatever success you experience will be short-lived unless you're able to use those successes to re-program your subconscious mind to be truly confident and live it out.

Which brings me back to the start of the book – working on your inner badass game. Plant a badass fruit and you'll continue reaping a masculine, badass fruit that includes such a manly, manly stroll! It's the kind of stroll that'll make people admire you – even if it's the first time they saw you – and women want to have you for dessert. Maybe even for the main course!

Think badass, be badass and walk badass manly! Out of the abundance of your inner manliness will your feet walk. There can be no other way – there can really be no other way!

#5: they often look beyond the crowd.

As they're walking, their mind is on their path.

They're not looking at everyone in the eyes to see what they think about them; they look straight ahead, as they're dominating their path.

The environment doesn't catch their attention, even if it's changing.

Remember, you're a badass! You supposed to exude confidence, charisma and an I-don't-care-if-you-care attitude. And what better way to do this than to act snobbish. Just keep in mind snobbish, not be a snob, which is not acknowledging the people who call you or approach you to talk or whatever.

Why is the snobbish look so damn high status? For one, it speaks of an internal sense of security and confidence that really, you're not interested in the goings on around you. You send the message that you don't need their approval to feel good about yourself. You're your own man and all you need's yourself to feel secure.

Another reason for its being high status is that it quietly sends this message: "You people aren't worth my attention. Your lives are probably as interesting as watching a goldfish swim in the aquarium. On the other hand, I'm so interesting and intriguing that I am very much intrigued and interested in myself! I'm so interesting and intriguing that you'll find me as such and you'll want to get to know me and initiate contact just so you can find

out what the mystery's all about! I won't vie for your attention –
you will vie for mine."

Third, the snobbish look makes people, specifically women,
excited to know you. If you're the type who always smile at just
about anyone in the room and always initiates the first contact,
you'll be sending a contradictory message to the ladies. Subtly,
this is what you'll be saying if you don't have this characteristic:
"Hi, I'm not that interesting, hence my consistent efforts to
always smile at you and initiate contact. I'm also not secure and
confident with myself, hence the need to always initiate contact
and look at everyone in my path. Please, somebody save me
from the banality of my existence! Have mercy on me!"

Alright, I may have exaggerated a bit there but my point is that
looking beyond the crowd often makes you more interesting and
badass!

Those were the five principles of a real, badass walk.

Every man has his own unique walking style, which can be trained and mastered with some easy tricks and tips.

Go ahead and prepare yourself, badass.

After reading the next chapter, your walk will never be the same!

Robert Moore

How to Walk Like a Real Badass - Make Sure She Finds Your Walk Sexually Attractive

I bet that in your mind, there is already a picture, a movie, a song, something that gives you the idea of a high status walk. It's as if you have Netflix in your mind and from it, you watch video clips of how James Bond, Dwayne "The Rock" Johnson and Hugh Jackman are used to walk.

You already know what it looks like. And so does your brain and your subconscious.

Right now, you need to give yourself the permission to walk like that.

Remember positive affirmations? This is one of the best times to use it! If your subconscious mind still isn't programmed to walk like a badass, say the words you want to be over and over and over until it sinks from your conscious mind to your subconscious mind. If you think it's already there, there's no harm in continuing to reinforce it! Remember we talked about making no room for the former, wussy self to be able to come crawling back in?

Say to yourself something like this: *"I'm a high status dude now. I see myself high status. From now on, I will walk like the most famous actors and leaders, because I LOVE being so dominant, charming and relaxed!"*.

First of all, in order to completely internalize the high status walk, you should start modeling someone who already gained this skill.

Model him until you start getting consistent results doing his way, and then innovate and add your own style in your walk.

Pick one or two walking models. Watch their movies, their interviews, try to catch every particular movement. Or they may be a couple of friends, someone you hang around with, and that will be even better, because you'll be in their environment and you'll learn this skill quickly.

Once a day, read through all the five principles of the badass walk you just read in the previous chapter.

Then pick your model and watch him walking for one minute, focusing and the five principles.

Then, practice modeling his walk for three minutes.

Repeat this sequence every day for one week.

Practice is key here, my action-taking friend! Practicing what you learned and observed by actually walking that way helps you reprogram your subconscious mind to exude, reflect and act out the new, badass nature inside of you. Think of it as the external internalization of the badass principles. The more you literally walk the talk, the more your talk becomes the walk!

And speaking of practice, I read in Malcolm Gladwell's best-selling book Outliers about a study whose conclusion includes you need to practice – on average – about 10,000 hours to master something, whether it's playing the electric guitar or hitting the baseball. I don't know about you badass, but 10,000 hours of walking seems a bit too much. It's like running 2,000 sub-5 hour marathons. That's insane! I may not have clocked my actual hours of practice but I can safely say that I didn't need to walk 10,000 hours to get the badass walk down to pat. It only took me 9,999 hours!

Kidding aside, the amount of time and practice needed to master the badass walk varies from person to person but I can assure you that it won't take you a lifetime!

There are ways to help make your "practice" walks more efficient and make you master the badass walk much faster. One is by getting the feedback of your closest female friends.

I wouldn't advise getting your male friends' advice because chances are, they don't have a clue – unless they're gay, in which case what attracts women attracts them as well. By getting their feedback, you enjoy the benefit of seeing yourself walk from another person's point of view. Further, since your main objective is to seduce and attract women, getting women's – or gays' – feedback is as close to the truth about how you're doing in your badass walk as possible.

If you don't have female friends (poor you) or even gay ones, don't despair! You can have the option of video recording yourself and watching against clips of people like Harvey Specter or Brad Pitt to see how far off or close you are to mastering the badass walk.

I personally practiced using Ryan Gosling as a model. I've never seen him walking without a purpose. He's always tall and open, his walk is smooth and controlled. And of course, women find him sexy and extremely high status.

Remember that even though practice doesn't make perfect, it can make you excellent at it.

Every time you walk, consciously practice excellence.

Even the first walk of your day, when all the mediocre guys go to the bathroom in a lazy, tired, flabby way, should be high status and powerful. Walk around the house for a few minutes, preferably in front of a mirror or a video camcorder. Feel, internalize and believe you are inhabiting the body of your role model, be it James Bond, Ryan Gosling or Matt Bomer in White Collar. Start your day right by practicing your badass walk!

What if you have a very poor memory? You can take memory enhancing supplements or get more sleep. If they still don't work or if you don't have the luxury of time for more sleep, you can put a note near your bed, in an area where you will immediately see it. That way, you won't have any excuse not to start your day the badass way.

Always trust the process, and the results will come. It's exactly how it's supposed to be: you're a high status man now. Do not listen to the mediocrity around you and keep going on your path.

Visualize yourself walking on the streets in a dominant, relaxed... awesome way. Visualization can be very, very helpful in helping you reprogram your subconscious mind to naturally make you walk badass! In fact, it's one of the most popular – and rightly so – techniques for producing effective and lasting personal change. Why?

It's because the subconscious mind – unlike the conscious – can't tell the difference between real and imagined experience. You don't believe me, bro? Alright, check this out.

Can you consciously make your penis as hard as a rock simply by wanting it to, without any physical assistance whatsoever? I doubt. It's because unlike your hand that you can control with your subconscious mind, you can't make your junior sausage stand up at will. Now try this...

Think of the hottest woman you know and in vivid detail, visualize in your mind that she's giving you head and that she's doing it like she's hadn't had anything to eat in the last 3 weeks – she's that hungry for your wiener! Can you feel your junior sausage rise up to the challenge? I assume yes. Mine just did as I'm writing this...dang!

And that, my dear friend, is the power of visualization. Your subconscious mind wasn't able to decipher that your visualization isn't real...that's it's all just a grand attempt by your conscious mind to deceive it into making your cock-a-doodle-doo rise up. It responded as if it were real. And the proof of the pudding is in the rising, in this case.

Can you imagine if you reinforce your actual practices with your mental practice sessions using visualization? In fact, you don't have to. Countless studies have shown the power of mentally rehearsing what are otherwise physical performances – be it sports or playing a musical instrument. Their results showed that the improvements in actual, physical performance weren't significantly different between mental and physical rehearsals. In fact, some of them even showed that the lethal combination of actual and mental (visualization) practices significantly improved performance compared to using just either of the two methods. If professional athletes and musicians utilize visualization to supplement actual, physical practice, why shouldn't you in your badass walking efforts?

Before we part ways, I just want to say that I can't overemphasize enough the importance of practicing what you learned here. By combining actual practice with visualization, you are effectively reprograming your subconscious mind to become more and more badass. Practice, visualize and then let this vision manifest in your reality!

Robert Moore

Conclusion

When you have a high status body language, people conclude that you are in CONTROL of your own reality.

So, as you learned in this book, be comfortable first; take up your space and let your body language be powerful and dominant. This will let other people around you feel better, it will make them relax and be comfortable too: that's your goal as a high status leader, so be an example.

Remember this, my badass friend:

The body follows the mind, but the mind follows the body even more.

Having a high status body language will make you have a high status mindset all the time.

That's the real strength and the main benefit of displaying a badass body language.

In order to train your new walk, make it a conscious practice all the time, following the sequence you can find in the relative chapter.

And now imagine: your body language will be great, girls will be attracted by your powerful positions and ways of carrying yourself.

They will come to talk to that handsome guy and... your voice sounds like crap.

That's really a bad situation. Body language is extremely important, but unfortunately it can't do anything about a crappy voice.

That's why I dedicated a whole book on Voice Training.

And since YOU deserve a powerful, dominant voice... I've put a preview of my book Voice Training in the next chapter.

You're welcome man.

Don't miss this opportunity.

Finally, if you enjoyed this book, then why don't you leave a review on Amazon, just like all the other customers did? Your opinion is important in order to make this guide better and better. I really appreciate your feedback!

Robert Moore

Robert Moore

Preview Of Voice Training

Why A High-Status Voice Is So Powerful

During your life, you probably have been in different social situations and encounters. I mean, you heard so many voices in your life, so many speeches, in TV, in real life or on the phone.

You probably learned that no matter what you're saying or what you're doing, if it's coming through a crappy voice no one wants to hear. Someone can be telling the most amazing story but if it sounds f***ing annoying, you simply don't want to hear.

On the other hand, if someone has a FANTASTIC, commanding, powerful voice, and he's also telling an interesting story, you will probably want to hear.

The question is: why?

What makes a high status voice so powerful?

Why it's so attractive and influential?

Reason #1:

Voice is one of your most important sub-communications, that lets people know what status level you perceive yourself as.

Now, read that phrase at least three times. And then write it down. Then read what you wrote. You're welcome.

And from now on, remember this: "the world tends to accept the judgment YOU place on yourself".

If you think you're confident and powerful and you're making it clear to the world, then it will quickly accept the fact that you are awesome.

In contrast, if you perceive yourself as someone not that fantastic, or not that worthy, the world will believe the same.

So, if someone hears your voice, he or she is getting really quickly what status level you perceive yourself as.

Are you talking aloud because you think you're worthy and people should hear you? Or are you talking quieter, because you don't believe in yourself, in your value?

Are you talking at your own pace or are you conditioned by outside events?

Are you directly participating in a proactive way? Or maybe are you just standing there, without making your opinion clear?

So, henceforth let people perceive your inner power.

Reason #2:

Being a good communicator is, in general, powerful on its own.

It shows that you're used to people listening to you, being affected by you and by your words.

Speaking with a clear, commanding voice is a display of your social intelligence.

Who else in history had great voices? Political leaders, world-class actors, every leader in general. When you exhibit your inner badass voice, people tend to associate leadership qualities and potential with you.

Think about a guy who is telling an interesting story to his friends, and they are all listening with rapture, looking at him with their mouths open.

A good communicator ALWAYS stands out: imagine yourself going to a business meeting with a fantastic, commanding vocal presence and being recognized as the most valuable, powerful person in the group.

Probably you'll be recognized as a leader, because most people nowadays have mediocre voices.

So, understand that your vocal expression is a fundamental aspect of your personal development. A great vocal projection shows that you're used to people listening and loving the words that you say, because you're high status.

If you're really on point with your words, with a loud, clear, commanding voice, then people will think that simply this isn't new for you.

You can have a supercar, you can own a nice house, or you can know that VIP. But these are not real high status signals. They can be fake.

On the other hand, you can't fake your voice. If yours is deep and powerful, everyone you meet will feel that on a subconscious level.

The 5 Traits Of A Powerful Voice

What makes a voice powerful and high status?

Every commanding, powerful voice has five traits:

1.   It is authoritative

2.   It is clear

3.   It is unaffected

4.   It is interesting

5.   Often breaks rapport

If you want to really make your voice stand out in a powerful way, then go ahead and check the whole book out, Voice Training, on Amazon.com.

I will explain to you the five traits of a high status voice, I will show you the exercises I personally used in order to strengthen my mouth muscles and the secrets used by Hollywood actors in order to make their vocal expressions the most attractive on this planet.

YOU DESERVE A POWERFUL VOICE, my badass friend.

Just imagine yourself at a business meeting: you will be the most valuable guy there, because your voice will be so **STRONG** and **COMMANDING**. Everyone will be raptured by your words.

Political leaders and actors were not born with a powerful voice, they **TRAINED** it up to that point. In fact, you don't have a quiet voice, you simply trained it that way.

Now it's time to train it the other way around!

Go get it NOW.

Check Out My Other Books!

Eye Contact Training - How To Attract And Seduce A Woman, Increase Your Confidence And Become A Leader

What if I told you that with some easy, powerful exercises you can get a deep, high status eye contact in just a few days? It would change your life, right?

Well, IT CHANGED MY LIFE. When you can handle the tension of a deep eye contact with everyone, you feel invincible. When you can handle the eyes of your boss, staring directly at them with confidence, then you'll stop feeling like his slave.

And with girls... damn, keeping a high status eye contact with girls it's completely GAME-CHANGING.

The techniques I show you in this book will make them chasing for your attention: they are so powerful, that even HOLLYWOOD ACTORS use them.

People will start doing things for you, they will start looking to you for decisions and, for the most part, they'll simply do whatever you say.

Remember this, my badass friend:

"With great eye contact comes great power, and with great power comes a lot of pussy."

Now, here is what you'll discover in Eye Contact Training:

Why a high status Eye Contact is so important for your life...

What a high status Eye Contact exactly is: one simple trick to deep, powerful, relaxed eye contact...

How to command complete control of your eyes and your attention: this SCREAMS high status to anybody watching...

Eye Contact Training: how to OWN your internal tension - Specific practices and exercises to train you how to handle tension inside and outside...

... and much more!

Confidence Training: - Become An Alpha Male by Mastering Your Confidence, Self Esteem & Charisma

Confidence is one of the most important traits to master if you want to succeed in your life.

While you decided to bet on yourself, most men out there are going to continue on their boring lives, controlled by their emotions, like weak little leaves in the wind. You will not.

You're meant for greatness, and I hope this guide will help you reach your goals and transform your life.

In fact, for some guys, mastering their emotions and becoming truly confident will be their graduation from little children to ALPHA MALES. Because from now on, your emotions will work for you, instead of the other way around.

I'm talking about pure, unshakable confidence, which means untouchable indifference and emotional mastery at its finest.

So you can finally start ENJOYING and LIVING LIFE like the king you know you are, staying cool, calm, and collected, no matter what life throws at you.

I'm talking about you finally being able to ask that girl out that you've so desperately wanted to.

I'm talking about you walking straight up to your boss' office and demanding that raise that you deserve (the right way) and getting it within the snap of a finger.

I'm talking about you finally being able to take on ANYTHING that life throws at you, without even flinching.

I'm talking about complete and utter state control over your emotions, for good.

I'm talking about laser-like focus, allowing you to get done in a day what most people get done in a month.

Let's get you going – you're ready for this!

www.ingramcontent.com/pod-product-compliance
Lightning Source LLC
Chambersburg PA
CBHW071208280526
45787CB00002B/603